CANYON
COUNTRY
CLIMBS

KATY CASSIDY AND EARL WIGGINS

CANYON
COUNTRY
CLIMBS

PRUETT **P** PUBLISHING COMPANY
Boulder, Colorado

Pruett Publishing Company, 2928 Pearl Street, Boulder, Colorado 80301

First Edition
1 2 3 4 5 6 7 8 9

Printed in Japan

Library of Congress Cataloging-in-Publication Data

Cassidy, Katy, 1960–
    Canyon country climbs / Katy Cassidy & Earl Wiggins.
        p.   cm.
    ISBN 0-87108-766-9
    1. Rock climbing—Utah—Guide-books.   2. Utah—Description and travel—1981– —Guide-books.   I. Wiggins, Earl, 1957–   .
II. Title.
    GV199.42.U8C37   1989
    796.5′223′09792—dc19   89-3672
                                                               CIP

Design by Jody Chapel, Cover to Cover Design, Denver, Colorado.

THIS BOOK IS DEDICATED TO:

Our loving parents
Milt and Mary Ellen, Joe and Eleanor

CONTENTS

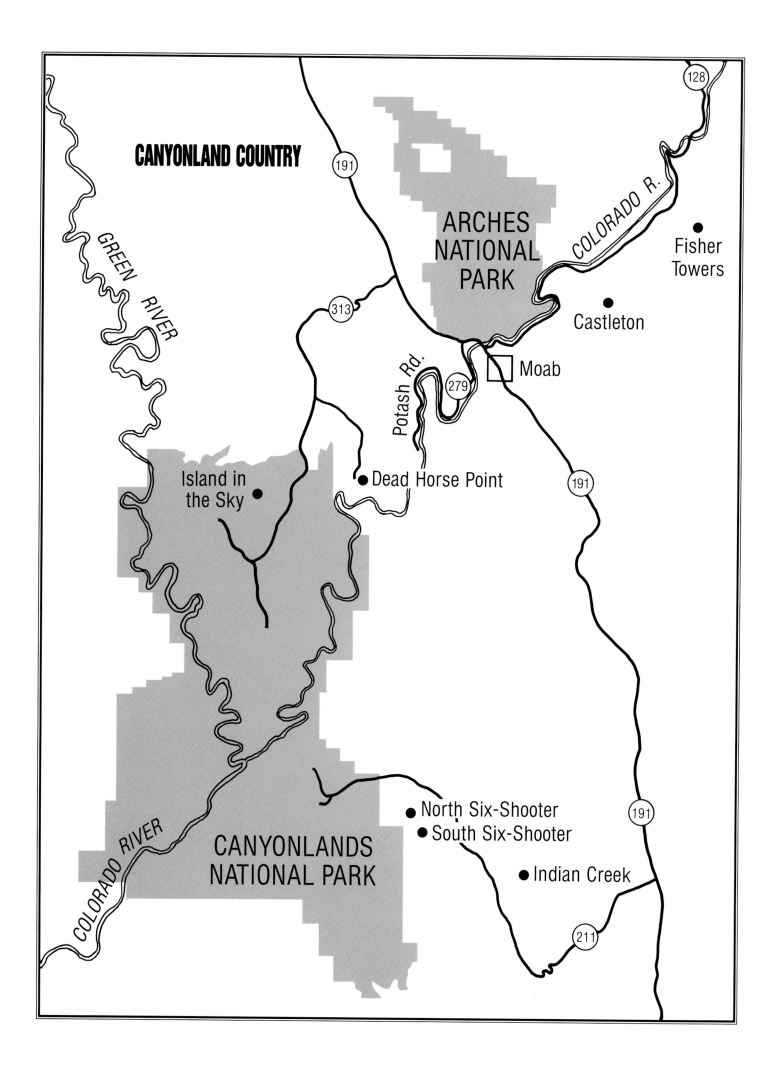

ROCK TYPES

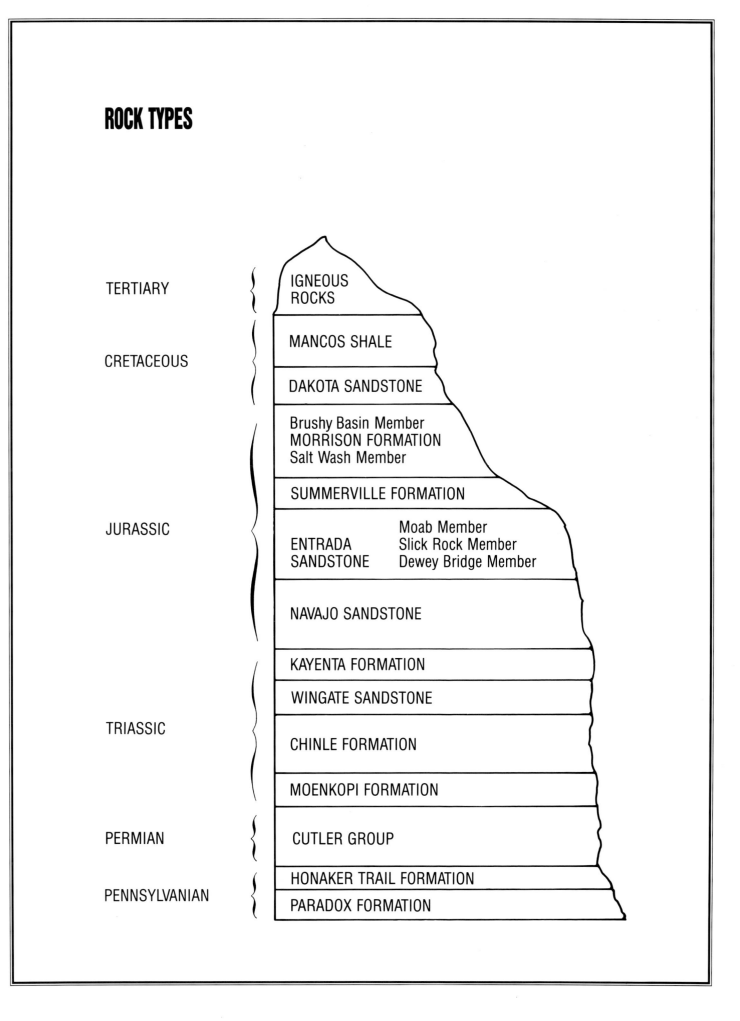

TERTIARY

IGNEOUS ROCKS

MANCOS SHALE

CRETACEOUS

DAKOTA SANDSTONE

Brushy Basin Member
MORRISON FORMATION
Salt Wash Member

SUMMERVILLE FORMATION

JURASSIC

ENTRADA SANDSTONE — Moab Member
Slick Rock Member
Dewey Bridge Member

NAVAJO SANDSTONE

KAYENTA FORMATION

WINGATE SANDSTONE

TRIASSIC

CHINLE FORMATION

MOENKOPI FORMATION

PERMIAN

CUTLER GROUP

HONAKER TRAIL FORMATION

PENNSYLVANIAN

PARADOX FORMATION

FOREWORD

When I first climbed in the desert in 1960, I was frightened by the softness of the rock and the loneliness of the pinnacle. Accidents seemed more likely because of the bad rock, and more serious because of the absence of other people. After that first climb I stayed away from desert rock until 1962 when Layton Kor and Huntley Ingalls asked me to join them for a warm-up climb on the Bell Tower in Colorado National Monument and then for an attempt on the biggest of the Fisher Towers, the Titan, near Moab.

On those climbs I discovered even more disadvantages to desert climbing. We had strong winds, and the dust and sand got into everything. I also learned that the desert can be very cold, and sometimes very wet.

But I also became aware of the attractions of desert climbing. The views were grand. There were spectacular and unexplored summits. The loneliness was both scary and exciting. Climbing on solid rock in Eldorado Springs was fun, but going to a remote desert tower meant uncertainty and high adventure. "What will we do if the rock becomes more mud than rock?" "What protection will work?" "How do we retreat?" "Can we even find a route?" In the end I weighed my anxiety against the attractions and continued to climb in the desert.

The high desert is unique and exotic. To someone from Europe or Japan, or from more temperate parts of the United States, the desert of Utah is as foreign as another planet. There are unusual land forms, not only towers but arches, buttes, mesas, and—most intriguing of all—deep and narrow canyons that promise fabulous discovery. I loved the approach to the Mystery Towers. I had seen them from the top of the Titan in the spring of 1962 and again in 1966, but I could see no way to get to them even though they were only a half mile east of the Fisher Towers. Bill Forrest obtained a set of stereoscopic aerial photos. We were delighted to see that a side canyon led from Onion Creek to the towers. We followed that very narrow canyon into the sandstone maze until it opened to show us the three unclimbed towers.

Recently a friend led me up a winding trail through a barren, rocky gap to a hidden valley west of Moab. Steep red walls rose on either side of a flat meadow covered in blue-green grass with clusters of yellow flowers. Clouds were low, covering the tops of the canyon walls. It was a hidden place of great beauty, one version of Shangri La. This would have been reward enough, but the meadow led us to a rock wall covered with dozens of petroglyphs. The most exciting were long lines of figures, human and animal. Some of the humans had shields, some were ghostly, some had animal heads. They were intermingled with bighorn sheep and deer. Some stood alone and some seemed to dance in long processions.

Petroglyphs, cliff homes, and pottery shards are messages from a mythic past, reminders that the desert was home to societies far different from our own. The timeless quality of the desert makes us feel that the ancient ones are close.

On a more earthly level we often find flowers that are startling in their beauty, thrilling because of the contrast between the flower and its surroundings of black brush and juniper. Many desert plants are lovely and shy; others are spiky and defensive.

The animals could be described in the same way. Most desert animals are elusive, but the tracks we see everywhere fire our imaginations. The birds are less shy. Hawks and eagles, wrens and magpies, go about their business with little regard for climbers.

Climbers went into the desert slowly. At first only a few unique individuals were lured by the power and mystery of the desert. Even in the fifties and sixties the few climbers who liked to lead on desert rock were thought of as supermen. The fact that Mark Powell or Harvey T. Carter or Kor or Forrest could climb a desert tower did not imply that we ordinary people could climb them. The average climber felt terror when he realized just how soft, how crumbly, desert sandstone can be.

Some of us learned to live with desert rock. We were mountaineers, and in the tradition of mountaineering we wanted exploration and we wanted to reach summits. The desert offered both possibilities. We climbed free as long as we could, but had no objection to using aid. The goal was to find a way to the top.

Today most desert climbers are not as interested in reaching summits. They go to canyon walls to climb difficult cracks that may or may not reach the top of the wall. Exploration for these climbers means expanding their own limits, or finding new and unclimbed cracks to work on and finally conquer. The social aspect of climbing is important in an area like Indian Creek, where on a spring weekend there may be as many as one hundred climbers. Just as good dancers who want to improve need and enjoy the company of other good dancers, so climbers are helped by their association with other climbers.

Because of the larger numbers of climbers in the desert in the eighties, some of the fear we felt in the sixties has disappeared. Climbing on soft sandstone has come to seem more normal. Even on remote towers there is some comfort in having more information and better equipment.

The desert will always be an inhospitable and dangerous place to climb. It will always be awesome in its rugged silence. But for those climbers who feel the magic of the desert there is lots of space and unlimited challenge.

GEORGE HURLEY
Conway, New Hampshire
May 1988

Indian Ruins *Katy Cassidy*

PREFACE

The canyon country of southeastern Utah is a landscape of vast mazes carved by eons of water and wind. The visual passage of time can be witnessed in this dynamic geography of ever-eroding sandstone. Breathtaking views saturated by earth tones, reds, yellows, greens, with smatterings of blues and purples, offer a feast for the eyes.

The orderly layering of sandstone sediments, each with its own characteristics, follows the rise and fall of geologic uplifts and faults. The topmost layers form miles of petrified sand dunes, rolling hills of pink, yellow, and orange striations. Whole sides of these slickrock hills have dropped away, leaving sheer rock faces. High on these faces huge grottos are formed, streaked black with seepage and lined with green ferns. On other cliffs, cascading bowls of rock pour into one another, draining the landscape above. These slickrock domes and fins slowly erode, exposing a multitude of caves and various other natural wonders. The most delicate structure created by erosion is the arch. The greatest span for an arch in this area is 291 feet—the longest in the world.

Talus slopes of red, brown, green, gray, yellow, and white rise steeply from the meandering Colorado River. Sometimes forming huge ridges rising thousands of feet, these gargantuan talus slopes fan out below the deep red, vertical cliffs of solid Wingate sandstone. The cliffs are topped by juniper-covered mesas. Apart from these mesas are countless free-standing buttes and pinnacles.

In contrast to the endless Wingate cliffs with their clean parallel fractures are the infrequent and crumbling, purple-brown fins and pinnacles of the Cutler formation. Formed by layers of mud and stone, towers found in this much older stratification gradually shrink in diameter toward their base, only to be left balancing precariously on thin plates of rock. That these structures still stand after a long stare, let alone after years of wind and rain, is amazing.

Thoughts of the desert conjure forbidding pictures of sand, rocks, and sparse patches of grasses or thorny plants. In places this desert certainly is spare of vegetation, as on the hills of slickrock and on certain windswept dunes where seeds are unable to take root. But despite the radical temperature changes of this harsh environment, the desert is lush with sturdy junipers, sage trees, and a variety of desert plants. A major reason this desert is able to propagate so well is its cryptogamic soil. This dark crust of soil is found throughout the desert area. It is composed of several species of mosses, lichens, fungi, and algae. This spongy surface absorbs moisture, traps seeds, and stabilizes soil, allowing seeds to sprout and grow, thus creating a vegetated area in an otherwise barren place. Cryptogamic soil is extremely fragile; one inch of growth takes between twenty-five and one hundred years. Care must be taken to avoid unnecessary trampling of this fragile earth. Walking up washes, along slickrock, or single file through the soil helps preserve the desert.

This is desert country. It can be seen around you, and felt in the hot sun beating down. A sunny nook sheltered from the wind can make a cold winter's day feel like spring. Likewise in the cool shade of a narrow canyon, escape can be found from the pelting rays of summer sun. During spring and autumn when the desert is most prone to rain and moderate temperatures, the land comes alive with a multitude of small, colorful flowers. Soon after the last sudden rains of autumn have filled the washes with torrents of muddy water, winter arrives. The contrasting colors of desert reds and a blanket of snow is a treasured winter sight.

This land of intense natural beauty was the home of the Anasazi and Fremont Indians, the Ancient Ones. The Anasazi dwelled here for approximately 700 years, from about A.D. 600 until about A.D. 1300, when they suddenly and mysteriously disappeared from the area. Abundant natural caves, offering respite from the intense seasonal temperatures, were homes for the Ancient Ones. In these caves as well as under large boulders and along cliffs, remains of walls built of flat stones and mud can be found. A few dwellings contain small corncobs, shards of pottery with geometric designs still visible, and perhaps a well-worn metate. A metate is a large, flat, thick stone with a dip worn into it from years of rubbing grains on it with a smaller hand stone. A sharp eye and a keen intuition will locate these artifacts, which blend into the landscape so well. More noticeable are the petroglyphs left by the Anasazi. Pecked in the rock are angular bodies, herds of

Desert in Bloom *Stewart Green*

deer, and other facets of life familiar to the Ancient Ones. There are thousands of these drawings throughout the canyonlands area.

Dinosaur footprints preserved in rock, a chunk of petrified wood found along a creek bed, these are evidence that this feeling of being connected to the long ago is more than just imagination. The desert, with its deep Indian history and bizarre geology, while humbling, also imparts a sense of adventure and exploration unequalled anywhere.

ACKNOWLEDGEMENTS

We would like to thank all those who helped bring this book into being. Though too numerous to list, their names appear throughout the following pages in quotes, anecdotes, vignettes, and photographs. This project would not have been possible without their time and energy.

We give our heartfelt thanks to the following people for their immense amount of encouragement and advice before and during the long months of compilation:

Kevin Cassidy   Jeff Lowe

Dick Dumais   Maggi Ryan

Stewart Green   Ed Webster

George Hurley   Lynda Wiggins

Jeff Long

Our deep appreciation is accorded those people who generously contributed to this book from the rich stores of their private experiences in the Utah desert, about which they have long maintained a public silence.

We are also grateful to the friendly people of Moab who made us feel welcome in their small town.

Last but not least we would like to express a very special thanks to our publisher, Jim Pruett, who pursued this creative endeavor from an idea to its final product.

CASTLE VALLEY

Seventeen miles east of Moab lies Castle Valley, a broad drainage cascading from the north end of the La Sal Mountains to the Colorado River several thousand feet below. Standing guard on the eastern border of this beautiful valley, halfway between the snowcapped mountains rising above and the canyon country below, are the magnificent spires and buttes known as Castle Ridge. Perched atop a thousand-foot scree cone, the imposing presence of Castleton Tower is the epitome of the classic desert spire. With Castleton guarding the south end and the Convent standing watch to the north, the Rectory, Nuns, and Priest all keep a silent vigil overlooking the desert unfolding below. These pinnacles stand naked, the last solid vestiges of a mesa that once was. Unlike the broad mesa-covered buttes of Indian Creek and Canyonlands, this ridge of exposed pinnacles, isolated on their private thrones, offers a 360-degree view.

The La Sals to the south rise skyward to an elevation of 12,000 feet. To the west, Castle Valley drops persistently toward the swollen Colorado River. To the east lie an intricate maze of arroyos depicting the toll of erosion through the centuries. To the north, the massive Fisher Towers loom high above the Colorado River as it begins its journey through this remarkable canyon country.

Castleton Tower and its neighbors offer the active climber an abundance of desert crack climbs and spectacular summits. These demanding climbs average three to four hundred feet in height. The solid Wingate sandstone towers have been the stage for many desert adventures.

It was a hot September day in 1961 when two Colorado climbers first came to investigate the then unclimbed menagerie. Layton Kor, a bricklayer by trade, and Huntley Ingalls, an astrophysicist, had climbed very little on the soft sandstone of the American Southwest. The overwhelming sight of Castleton Tower soaring above them sparked their sense of adventure. Though it was already late morning, they quickly packed their pitons and climbing ropes into their rucksacks and set off up the arduous scree pile toward the steep shaft of rock. Upon arriving at the base they chose the most obvious and striking line for their proposed ascent. To their surprise, the rock was reasonably sound and offered superb climbing. By late afternoon they had ropes fixed halfway up the tower. The evening was spent in anticipation of the following day's climb and virgin summit. Bright and early the next morning they were retracing their steps up the long scree cone. They ascended their fixed ropes and set off onto new terrain. Determination and technical proficiency rewarded the pair with the summit of Castleton by midday.

Before they could descend, they were engulfed by a fierce electrical storm. Kor, thinking about how exposed they were, came to the stunning realization that Castleton was very possibly the Earth's greatest natural lightning rod. Hanging perilously with static electricity buzzing through the air and deafening bursts of thunder exploding

Castle Ridge *Katy Cassidy*

Kor-Ingalls Route 5.9, Castleton Tower *Katy Cassidy*

4

Dan Stone leading the North Chimney 5.8, Castleton Tower *Charlie Fowler*

all around, Kor, like many climbers to come, was filled with dread.

Numerous climbers have been caught unaware by the fast-moving electrical storms prevalent in fall and spring. The towering massifs of Castleton and its neighbors attract the explosive weather. In 1972, Jim Dunn and Doug Snively were overwhelmed by an electrical storm just as they were completing the first ascent of the North Face. Snively recounts how vulnerable they felt: "Just below the top, my hair stood on end and the metal frames of my eyeglasses were buzzing and shocking my cheeks. It was way scary." Crouching low, they ran as fast as they could across the small summit to the descent route on the other side.

The day after Kor and Ingalls completed the successful climb of Castleton Tower, they joined forces with Fred Becky and Harvey Carter, two climbers who in the future would become notable desert pioneers. The team set out to find a route to the top of the Priest. Kor and Carter were able to gain the summit before the afternoon storm set in. While waiting for Kor to rappel to the ground, Carter was knocked unconscious by lightning. As everyone waited anxiously on the ground, Carter slowly regained consciousness and cleared his foggy head. After a couple of minutes he was able to continue to the ground.

Defeated by the storm for the rest of the afternoon, Becky was determined to return the following day so he also could stand atop the magnificent spire that resembles a praying priest. The indefatigable Kor joined Becky for yet another trip up the horrendous scree cone and the second ascent of the Priest.

Feeling slightly cheated by not being invited on the first ascent of Castleton Tower, Harvey Carter returned the following year with Cleve McCarty. The pair were determined to complete the climb all free, to one-up Kor and Ingalls. "Kor used a bolt for aid, and when we went there I made sure I did it free," Carter recalls. This fierce competition was to continue for the next decade.

After their rapid all-free ascent, the pair set their sights on yet another unclimbed summit. This time the weather was much more cooperative, and without the threat of an afternoon storm, they were able to sit and enjoy the summit of their chosen climb, the Rectory. Over the next several years, each of the unclimbed summits on Castle Ridge fell to Carter's endless drive to climb.

The years since the sixties have provided many climbers the opportunity to establish first ascents of their own. In the early seventies, Jim Dunn, with several different partners, climbed the two existing routes and added two others on Castleton

Carol Petrelli leading the fourth pitch of Jahman 5.10, Sister Superior
Earl Wiggins

Climbers on Jahman 5.10, Sister Superior *Earl Wiggins*

The Priest and the Nuns *Bob Rotert*

Larry Floyd following the last pitch of the West Face of the Priest
Peter Gallagher

Larry Floyd leading the unprotected 5.8 chimney pitch on the
original route on the Priest *Peter Gallagher*

9

Tower. Completing the sixth ascent of the original route with Stewart Green enticed Dunn to try the second ascent of the North Chimney. Unable to climb a second day in the unbearable heat, Green was replaced by Dan Porter. Porter was a high school friend who was camping with Green and Dunn. He had never climbed before but was quickly drafted for the project by Dunn. Following Jimmy "the Madman" Dunn up the sheer tower left Porter with recurring nightmares for years.

Returning two months later, Dunn completed the West Face with Stewart Green and Billy Westbay, taking two days. The climb took everything the threesome could muster. Green recalls, "Jimmy aided out over the overhang tying several large loose blocks together before beating pins all around them. Above that the crack became too wide to nail and Billy took over the lead. He fought for several hours to inch his way up the steep pitch." For protection, Westbay was stacking bongs endwise and gently tapping them into the crack. "None of us really believed they would hold a fall," Green recounts. Slowly the three made progress, and by the afternoon on the second day they were safely on top, having completed one of the hardest desert climbs of the era.

For several subsequent years, Castleton saw only repeat ascents of the established routes. Focus for first ascents was drawn to other parts of the desert. Indeed, many people felt Castleton had no new routes left to climb. Then in 1977 Ed Webster began a desert saga of first ascents that continues still. Not since Kor had one man shown such

boundless energy to climb. To Castleton, Webster added three new routes and made free ascents of two others. Castleton has seen over one thousand ascents, yet its neighbor the Rectory has seen only a handful. With numerous untouched lines yet to be climbed on the Rectory and Convent, the area has only slightly been explored.

Since Castleton was first climbed in 1961, climbers have experienced the sheer walls in all types of weather. The searing heat of summer, the subfreezing temperatures of winter, and the warm, sunny days of spring and fall are just a few of the many different conditions to be found. There are as many different types of adventures to be had as there are climbers to experience them. Each climber's adventures are personal mementos of friends and places that one visits. Life is made richer with each memory gained and each experience survived. The Castle Ridge holds many wonderful adventures to come for those climbers bold enough to venture forth.

Buck Norden on the summit of Castleton *Ed Webster*

Thunderstorms bearing down on Castle Valley *Charlie Fowler*

EARLY DESERT CLIMBING

Jim Dunn first introduced me to desert climbing in the Utah canyon country in September 1971. The day of our ascent of the Kor-Ingalls route on Castleton Tower, the sixth ascent of the spire, dawned clear and warm, portending another hot Utah day. We quickly ascended through cool shadows on the steep slopes west of the tower to the base of the rock. Our only route description was a hastily scrawled excerpt from our desert "Bible"—the 1970 issue of *Ascent* magazine. It read, in part: "The route lies near the right side of the rock as viewed from the road." Certainly straightforward enough.

We roped up below the south face and ascended broken chimneys and rubble-filled ledges to the steep off-width crux. Meanwhile, the rock was heating up, burning my feet through the soles of my RDs. The shade in the notch just below the summit was both welcome and invigorating. From there the summit was a short traverse upward. After signing the register, we felt in privileged company; the book read like a Who's Who of sixties climbing—Layton Kor, Huntley Ingalls, Harvey Carter, Cleve McCarty, Steve Roper, Chuck Pratt, Royal Robbins, and Pat Ament.

At that moment, we felt we were a new generation of desert climbers. We saw a whole new world of rock out there just waiting to be climbed, and all of it unknown to the climbing world.

STEWART GREEN

Harvey T. Carter Layton Kor

Jim Dunn Stewart Green

13

FISHER TOWERS

Ancient Arts *Katy Cassidy*

Twenty-three miles east of Moab, separated from the mesa they were once a part of, the majestic Fisher Towers rise to heights of nine hundred feet. The path leading through this maze of spires is spotted with symmetrical puffs of desert shrubs, sparse junipers, and spiny bushes. Scattered throughout the landscape are the remains of small mud pinnacles with frail necks bent under the burden of balancing cap rocks.

Steep walls with mud curtains, fluted chimneys, and undulating bulges soar overhead. Stone diving boards protrude from grotesquely twisted summits. Hovering close to the La Sal Mountains, the Fishers suffer from a year-round barrage of mountain storms. The dense yet thin layer of Moenkopi cap rock barely protects the much softer Cutler sandstone from torrential rains and heavy snows. During the spring and fall, towers appear and disappear in cloaks of whirling clouds left by the lingering storms. On clear afternoons, the Fisher Towers stand hauntingly handsome in dark reds, purples, and chocolates, waiting for sunset to ignite them into a powerful fiery inferno.

The allure of these mud spires has captured only a small fraction of climbers visiting the desert. Many come at least once to climb the tallest tower, the Titan, yet few return a second time. There are only a few minor all-free routes; the majority of climbs in the area are multi-day aid ventures. Due to the difficult nailing, taking a whole day to lead a single pitch is not uncommon.

Most climbers don't understand the appeal that climbers returning to the area find in the masochistic experience. To climb here is to submit oneself to several days of abuse, including fear, frustration, intimidation, and an all-encompassing grime. When touched, the dry mud veneer disintegrates to pebbles and grit, filling the air to the point of suffocation.

This grit quickly invades everything—eyes, teeth, nose, shirts, socks, and pants. Being continually covered with this grit often grates on a climber's nerves. A leader easily spends half his time wiping dust from his eyes, and the belayer is best clothed in rain gear for the constant shower of pebbles and dirt. Climbing equipment suffers even more. Ropes saturated with the grit will quickly cut grooves into carabiners during descents. Jumaring over the rounded bulges can quickly shred a rope. This shredding process has led to most parties leaving two ropes when fixing a single pitch, one to jumar and one for a safety. Using this method over an eight-day period in particularly bad weather, one first ascent party lost thirteen ropes despite constant care to tape rubber over worn areas.

Again it was Kor and Ingalls who first climbed here. In 1962, accompanied by George Hurley, they succeeded in establishing a route on the Titan. Standing at the base, they all had serious doubts about the feasibility of climbing the sheer mud tower. Driven by the knowledge that if they didn't try it, someone else would, they slowly ascended the monstrous tower, taking four days to complete the climb.

A few months after the success of Kor and his

Climbers on the initial pitches of the Sun Devil Chimney 5.9 A3, the Titan *Earl Wiggins*

Jim Nigro and Harvey Miller nailing thin mud seams. The Sun Devil Chimney V 5.9 A3, the Titan *Art Wiggins*

John Meyers following a chimney pitch on the Sun Devil route V 5.9 A3, the Titan *Art Wiggins*

team, Harvey Carter and Cleve McCarty climbed King Fisher, a smaller yet just as formidable tower. On a hot, windless day, Carter decided to try a different approach to the mud walls. Wearing crampons made for ice climbing, he started off the ground trying to free climb the blank start. Carter recalls, "There was so damn much mud, I thought it would work well. After twenty feet, I fell and landed in the sand at the base. I then gave up that idea and started bolting." Bolting proved to be much better, but subsequent parties have been able to pull out the bolts by hand due to years of surface erosion.

Carter's next attraction was a repeat of the Kor route on the Titan. George Hurley had already returned and done the second ascent, and Carter wanted to be sure he achieved the third. "I climbed with Paul Sibley down in the Four Corners, and we stopped by the Fishers coming home. I showed him the route I wanted to do with him on our next trip. He came back the very next weekend and did the damn thing without me," he recalls somewhat angrily.

In 1967, Carter interested Art Howells from Colorado Springs in climbing Cottontail Tower, the second highest in the area. Howells rounded up a large team, and the plan was made to start a few days ahead of Carter, who had to finish work and would join the group once they were firmly started on the climb. It was obvious to Carter that Howells and his team wanted to complete the climb before Carter could join them. But only he knew how involved the project really was. He was quite confident they would not get to the top before his arrival.

The group grew to seven in the last few days before leaving Colorado. They were all considerably younger than Carter, ranging in age from seventeen to twenty-three. Don Doucette, who was eighteen at the time, remembers, "We didn't have any big wall experience. It was only the second time we had climbed outside of the Colorado Springs area. The Fishers were deceptively large. When we got there we thought we would be able to climb it in a couple of days. We were so dumb, we didn't know what we were seeing!"

Carter arrived several days after the group had started the climb. He joined the team, and together they inched their way to the top. Six long days after starting the route, the climbers crowded onto the tiny summit. Though the route was attempted many times after that, the group's feat stood unrepeated for sixteen years.

The last pitch of the Finger of Fate route 5.7 A2, the Titan *Bob Rotert*

Gary Olsen on the scary traverse pitch, Finger of Fate route 5.7 A2, the Titan *Bret Ruckman*

Bego Gerhart at the famous diving board belay on Ancient Arts, 5.10 A0 *Earl Wiggins*

The second ascent of Cottontail was accomplished by Ed Webster on a different route. During three attempts, Webster was able to solo this complicated route up the jagged south ridge. On his second attempt, he spent three days climbing to within a hundred feet of the summit. He had been sleeping in a natural cave three hundred feet above the ground each night and working his way closer to the top each day. Leaving fixed ropes above his cave, he was able to quickly return to his high point each morning.

Late on the third day a major storm engulfed the towers, obscuring visibility and forcing Webster to retreat to his small cave. As the night wore on, the tiny enclosure turned into a quagmire of mud. Drenched and freezing, Webster survived the bitter cold night by singing at the top of his lungs.

With all of his ropes hanging above him, he was forced to retrieve two of them before being able to descend to the campground at the end of the road. Having been dropped off by a friend a week earlier, Webster was relying on another friend to pick him up. Already two days overdue, the friend never did show. Webster was fortunate that there was a young couple camping at the campground. Aghast at the sight of a mud-covered apparition standing in the rain outside their tent, the couple finally understood the screeching songs echoing through the towers the night before.

Through the seventies, Harvey Carter continued to pioneer routes in the Fishers, each one just a bit harder than the previous one. One very notable ascent was the Sun Devil Chimney. Carter took fourteen days to complete it in stormy spring

The final belay on Ancient Arts, 5.10 A0 *Bego Gerhart*

weather, and this route has become a classic. The steep mud walls offer superb climbing. Most parties currently fix two pitches, camp at the base, and with an early start, race for the summit hoping to descend before dark. With nine hundred feet of demanding and intimidating climbing, this is not always a successful plan.

On the fifth ascent of the route and probably the first attempt at this race-for-the-summit plan, John Myers and Art Wiggins found themselves reaching the top at dark. They descended one pitch to a large ledge to evade the wind. With no sleeping bags or even jackets, it promised to be a long, cold night. Wiggins recalls Myers wanting to burn the only bush on the ledge to stay warm. Being somewhat environmentally conscious, Wiggins argued with him about destroying the poor bush.

As Myers got his small campfire going and Wiggins wrapped himself in ropes, the argument came to an abrupt end, each angry with the other. "I dozed off in my cocoon of ropes for a few hours and awoke shivering, stiff, and frozen. At that point I crawled over to John and his warm fire, bringing my own meager offering of twigs." Wiggins recounts, "A few years later, John and I again returned to that ledge on a descent from another climb. With a big grin John pointed at the healthy bush we had ravaged that long night."

The eighties brought a host of new routes to the mud walls of the Fishers. An amazing young man named Jim Beyers soloed seven major routes, six of which were first ascents. His expertise in thin nailing provided routes significantly harder than the previously established ones. Bold runouts

Sunset striking the Fisher Towers *Katy Cassidy*

on hooks, rurps, and bashies have distinguished these as extremely serious routes. Says Beyers, "The reason I liked climbing in the Fishers was because it is so scary."

Climbers simply can't avoid having adventures when climbing in the Fisher Towers. The storms can turn gritty mud walls into oozing, dripping, flowing curtains. High winds, common in the area, have been known to literally blow climbers off the rock. Mud seams offer unique if not altogether terrifying nailing. Sometimes unable to nail certain sections, a climber will be forced to free climb up crumbling columns and over loose blocks, frantically digging fingernails into the soft rock. This can quickly lead to mental exhaustion.

For some, perhaps the abundance of critters is the worst part. Bivouacing climbers have been known to stay up all night fighting off droves of suspected Cone Nose Kissing Bugs. These small bloodsucking bugs are known to carry a variety of diseases. One climber, bivouacing on the Titan, awoke to find a large spider on his face. Before he could instinctively flick it off, the spider had time to bite his eye. Within minutes the eye had swollen shut, and the climber was forced to descend and seek medical help. While soloing a new route, one brave climber was forced to battle an upset scorpion one-handed for several terrifying minutes while holding precariously onto a mud block with the other.

Having seen large cat tracks on his approach to the River Tower, Jim Beyers questioned his decision to solo a difficult new route he later named Savage Master. "That was kind of scary to be soloing and wondering if I was going to ground out. I could just picture dragging myself out of there with broken legs and having to fight off a mountain lion."

It is facing this combination of difficulties that repels some climbers yet attracts others. The handful that return again and again have found that the trials and humiliations are rewarded with spectacular summits and stupendous views. The adventures experienced in the Fisher Towers are unlike any others. With memories etched deeply for decades to come, climbers who have ventured into the Fishers will bear the influence of such perverse forays.

Peter Gallagher on Run Amok V 5.9 A4, Echo Tower *Art Wiggins*

Ed Webster on the first ascent of Brer Rabbit VI 5.9 A4, Cottontail
Stewart Green

THE TITAN

The first time I saw the Titan I was utterly mystified. How had Kor and his friends climbed this thing? Chuck Pratt and I wandered around the tower for an hour, scraping the mud curtains with our fingernails and straining our necks looking at the overhangs and gargoyles. We were used to Yosemite's clean, continuous, and *obvious* crack systems, and here we found the exact opposite: dirty, disconnected systems that we could follow for only a few hundred feet before they petered out in blank walls and overhangs.

Luckily, we had no plans on that trip to climb the monster. But six years later Pratt and I found ourselves back at the base, egged on by Royal Robbins, who apparently regarded the Titan as just another climb. Our threesome was ultra-experienced, with dozens of grade VIs to our credit. But we had learned not to take *any* climb lightly, and we were all more nervous than usual while roping up.

I well remember the feelings of awe and fear that spring day, but of the ascent itself I recall little. The routefinding was easy, a surprise to me, but the wall was even steeper than it had appeared. We dangled with apprehension in our belay seats from odd-looking anchor bolts on occasion, hoping Kor had been patient while drilling the holes. Red dust permeated every piece of clothing and equipment, and our eyes burned. The leader took an hour and a half to lead a pitch, but the cleaner and the hauler were up in twenty minutes. No one complained about overdriven pins. By dusk we were only a few pitches from the top, as planned, and the bivy ledge was like all of them: comfortable and huge at sundown, hard and tiny and repulsive at dawn.

Clouds covered the morning sun. Isn't that pretty, we thought. Within the hour a steady drizzle dampened our spirits and clothing, but we never considered going down; we had worked far too hard the previous day.

One of the upper pitches was mine, and it was perhaps the most spectacular desert lead I've done. The wind whipped my slings about as I swung my way from bolt to piton to bolt. The rain was hardly a consideration. Heading up that prow, I felt thrilled by the position and my calmness.

While signing the summit register, we noticed that the clouds were darkening further; they had also obscured the La Sals. Time to be off.

To put it mildly, the descent was not enjoyable. For one thing, Royal took immediate and total control of the rappel setups, a task for which I usually volunteered before anyone else could. It wasn't that I didn't trust the fellow; it was simply that I wanted to be in charge of my own fate. I felt like a sheep—or a client! But obviously I couldn't say a word to the Master. So I sat back and slithered over the edge when so ordered. The rappels were endless, difficult, and scary.

More galling, however, was the wet, red mud that soon covered ropes and clothing. We had wondered how the veneer of mud-rock curtains had formed on the Fisher Towers; now we saw first-hand as mud oozed like lava down the rock. Our nostrils and ears and lips were hilariously red and filthy. Two of our wives were waiting below, and I imagined their look of disgust when they saw our bodies. I also pitied the person who cleaned the showers at the KOA campground in Moab.

Preoccupied with the drizzle and the mud, and still sullen at being a sheep, I failed to check my carabiner brake system from time to time. As I dismantled the system after the final rappel, I was horrified to see that two carabiners had been sawed a third of the way through by the abrasive action of the rope and mud. Another few rappels and I would have probably heard, as my last sound on earth, the rending and tearing of metal and rope.

Steve Roper

Kor bolts on the Finger of Fate route, the Titan
Bret Ruckman

ARCHES
NATIONAL PARK

One hundred fourteen square miles of varied landscape—delicate arches, precariously balanced rocks, and a proliferation of curious rock formations—this is Arches National Park. Shades of red, yellow, and orange dominate this fanciful display of erosion. Just five miles northwest of Moab is the entrance to this bizarre wonderland.

From the Colorado River at the southern border of Arches, the winding main road through the park starts at 4000 feet and gains elevation rapidly. Sheer walls, some towering over 550 feet, rise abruptly from the desert floor. Slickrock towers, like statues of human and animal forms, capture and hold the imagination. These imposing formations, with their numerous crack systems, are protected by a skirt of featureless rock at their base.

North of these walls is Courthouse Wash, the main drainage for the southern end of Arches National Park. Courthouse Wash has carved its own deep side canyon through massive slickrock domes on its way to empty into the Colorado River below.

Beyond Courthouse Wash, the Great Wall, an unbroken wall of rock contouring in and out of shallow side canyons, heads north, gradually deteriorating into numerous fins as the elevation increases. Here the topography changes. Formations shrink in size to about 100 feet in height. Numerous arches appear, and the landscape becomes riddled with the small, gnarled pinnacles of the Dewey Bridge member of Entrada sandstone.

This is the highest point of Arches National Park, at 5500 feet.

Looking north one can see the Fiery Furnace, an intricate maze of fins and pinnacles colored deep red and topped in white. The Fiery Furnace stands ready to consume any careless hiker who should happen to lose his way. Farther north and west, ridges of slickrock fins offer views in all directions as they ride the swells of wide open valleys. On the far horizons are the last of the slickrock towers, the Marching Men to the west and the brooding, solitary Dark Angel to the north.

Arches National Park is exceptionally exposed to winds, and there is little rainfall. Most local storms are attracted to the La Sal Mountains, lightly dusting Arches on their way by. This dry, windswept climate of Arches is what allows such spectacular shapes to occur. A wetter climate would dissolve the soft, sandy Entrada sandstone of Arches into indiscriminate blobs. This land of physical improbabilities on the tenuous edge of collapse is endlessly fascinating to the imaginative mind.

Irene and Fred Ayres first started coming to the desert in the early 1930s. On one trip Irene and her brother struck out for this place they'd heard about called Arches.

"The roads weren't paved, you didn't really know where you were going. You just took your compass and headed off, taking roads that went in that direction," Irene recalls.

To the Ayres the desert was hot and thirsty, and a very wonderful place. Populated mostly by deer

''Double O'' Arch *Katy Cassidy*

Alison Sheets on the first ascent of Hamburger Hell 5.10 A2 *Katy Cassidy*

Kyle Copeland on the first ascent of Bugger's Banquet 5.9 A3, Sheep Rock *Charlie Fowler*

and smooth, exciting rock formations, Arches lured Fred and Irene back for several return trips to climb the arches and explore.

In 1955 the Ayres succeeded in reaching the top of both spans of Double Arch. This unorthodox climb required a few false leads to start with, 400 feet of rope (some to climb with, the rest for fixing lines on this complicated route up cracks, across fins, and down overhangs), and a ten-foot log barely long enough to span the deep, vertical walled chasm between the double arches. Balancing carefully, the Ayres shimmied across this log from one sloping, rounded arch to the next.

Fred and Irene adhered to the climbing traditions of the times, being conscientious about removing all their pitons and only bolting as a last resort. Even so, the park service has since decided the arches are too fragile to be climbed, deeming their ascents illegal. Several years passed before climbers again appeared at Arches.

On a frigid winter day in 1964 Layton Kor visited Arches with Bob Bradley and Charlie Kemp. They were determined to climb one of the numerous untouched towers. Armed with a November 1962 issue of *National Geographic*, featuring Kor's climb of the Titan, the trio approached the rangers of Arches to request permission to climb. It was regarded as an unusual request by the National Monument bureaucracy. No one had previously wanted to climb anything other than the arches themselves, something that had been recently forbidden. Yet here were three scruffy young men seeking sanction to attempt one of the many soft sandstone towers.

The rangers' first response was negative. No one had wanted to climb the towers before, why

Soft rock *Earl Wiggins*

34

should they start now? Yet, an article in *National Geographic*, worshipping Kor's climbing talents, carried a lot of clout. After several hours of diplomatic negotiations, Kor was able to secure permission to attempt a smaller formation. Kor is unable to remember why he chose the name Argon Tower. "Argon is a gas. Maybe we had a gas problem on the climb," he jokes.

The climbing was difficult, as was to be expected in the desert. The surprising aspect to Kor was how sandy and sugary the rock was. He had thought the Fisher Towers were dirty, but at least there the rock had been good and solid underneath the mud covering. Here the rock was rounded and extremely soft. Pin placements and anchors were questionable, and the constant light sifting of sand was not to his liking. Kor found nothing in the experience to entice him to return. Although few routes are crisp and clean in Arches, those that do exist are superb climbs, but they are usually quite short. However, the true flavor of Arches climbing is not afforded in these clean endeavors. The true Arches experience is characterized by soft rock, rounded cracks, sandy surfaces, and gripping pitches. It is not uncommon to fill a drilled ⅜-inch hole with a 1- or 1¼-inch angle, especially on the weathered summits where the consistency is more that of table sugar than rock.

Burdened by years of rules and regulations inhibiting climbing, Arches has much to offer the modern climber looking for first ascents. Though most of the larger towers have been climbed, multitudes of smaller virgin summits await future ascents. With easy approaches, spectacular scenery,

and limitless route potential, this area would seem to be attractive to climbers. Yet the gritty, soft rock keeps all but the most perverse away.

Climbing in Arches features both aid and free routes. Many of the free routes were originally aid lines. In the sixties very little was climbed here. A few of the desert pioneers felt obligated to come for at least one visit, though like Kor, most never returned after their initial ventures. Kor, Pratt, Robinson, Kamps, Rearick, Steck, Roper, and Carter came, sampled the climbing, and moved on to other more promising regions. The visits were short, but many of their routes remain to this day as quality soft-rock climbs. Dark Angel, Argon, the Three Gossips, and Buccaneer Rock all offer an ideal Arches experience.

The seventies were almost as quiet as the preceding decade. Though a few free climbs were finally established by Jim Dunn, Jim Newberry, Scott Gilbert, and Ron Olevsky, the emphasis remained on aid climbing and towers. In 1972 Muff Cheney and Jon Pease established yet another route on Argon Tower. Nobody seemed surprised that there were three routes on Argon and countless surrounding towers with no routes. "Argon was the most beautiful and most feasible," Cheney remembers. "It was what immediately caught everyone's eye."

Those who climbed with Jon Pease in the seventies knew he had a habit of talking to himself constantly while climbing. Large in stature, Pease was a frightening prospect to belay, especially from spooky desert anchors. His constant deep baritone monologue, usually portending doom, certainly had Cheney on edge. "He was up there telling

Bret Ruckman on the second pitch of the Kor route 5.9 A3, Argon Tower *Ruckman collection*

Peter Gallagher and Bego Gerhart on the first ascent of the South Gossip 5.11 A0, the Three Gossips *Earl Wiggins*

Charlie Fowler on the first ascent of Queen for a Day A2+, Queen Victoria Rock *Alison Sheets*

himself how bad his pins were and trying to free climb around the particularly scary placements. Groaning and moaning, talking constantly about falling, and all the time thrashing upwards, he would plead with the rock one minute and threaten it the next. I just kept checking and rechecking my anchors."

There was an explosion of activity in the park in the 1980s when rules and regulations were relaxed. Countless routes both free and aid were established. Most of the large unclimbed towers were at once targeted. One after another they were scaled, often with much difficulty. There were new routes added to the Three Gossips and other towers, as well as repeat ascents of Argon. Todd Gorden and Dave Evans were close to the top of Argon in 1984 when Gorden pulled off an enormous hold above his head. The hold instantly disintegrated and filled his open mouth as he gasped in horror. Digging the sand out of his mouth with his fingers, Gorden was glad the hold had disintegrated; a solid block would certainly have knocked out all of his teeth.

In 1986 and 1987 Charlie Fowler became a driving force. Teaming up with various partners, he accomplished many fine ascents on almost all of the Park Avenue towers. His drive to climb is evident in the astonishing number of first ascents in this area. His most notable ascent, Zenyatta Entrada, was accomplished over several days using a soloing system, yet being accompanied at times by old-timers Lin Ottinger and Eric Bjørnstad. Perhaps the most beautiful climb in Arches, this route follows incipient cracks for 500 feet up a vertical prow on the Tower of Babel.

In 1987 and 1988 the expert solo climber of the decade, Jim Beyer, established A5 routes on Organ Rock and Tower of Babel. Beyer's use of bashies, hooks, and rurps on routes following nonexistent seams up overhanging walls has established him as a master of the sport. On his Tower of Babel route he fell one hundred feet head first and stopped thirty feet above the ground. Jim was not particularly upset about the fall and chance of getting hurt; he was more perturbed that he had lost time and would have to reclimb the pitch.

Climbing in Arches is a unique experience. The softness of the rock demands positions, moves, protection, and anchors that are not needed in other areas. The pristine beauty, outrageous landscape, and breathtaking views add a calming quality to any climbing project. Combining challenging climbing and spectacular scenery, Arches is a wonderful and virtually untouched playground.

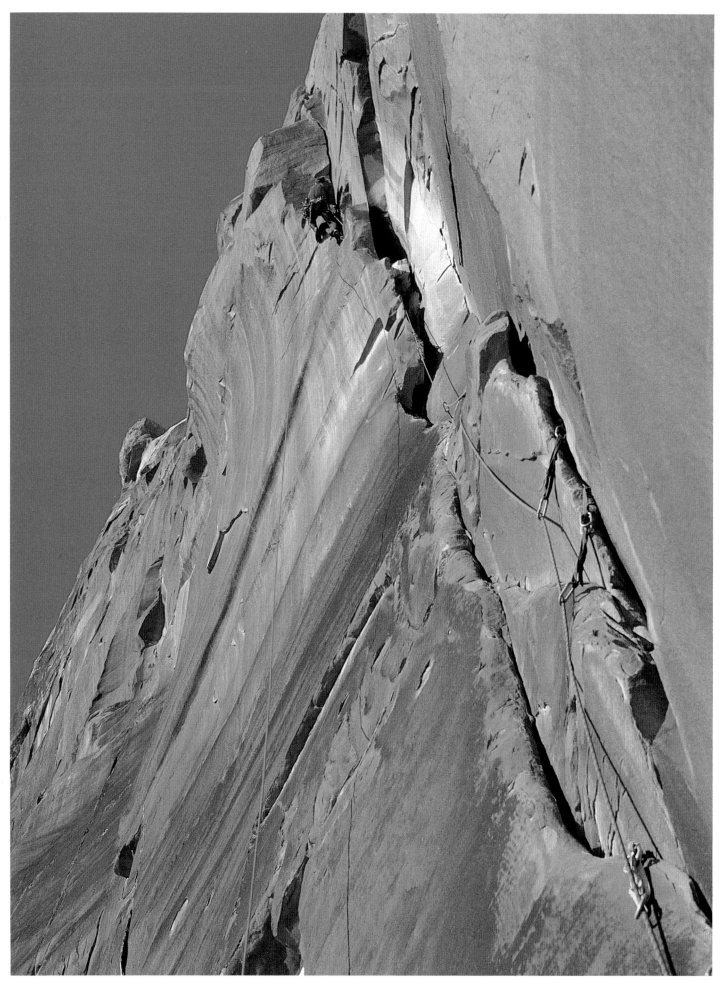

The first ascent of Off the Couch 5.11 *Katy Cassidy*

Jim Beyers on the first ascent of Wankers Away A5, Tower of Babel
Earl Wiggins

Sonja Paspal on Chinese Eyes 5.9, the Great Wall *Earl Wiggins*

Peter Gallagher on Mr. Sombrero 5.11, the Great Wall *Earl Wiggins*

Dark Angel *Katy Cassidy*

Climbing party on Dark Angel original route 5.9 A0 *Bego Gerhart*

Climbers on the ever popular Owl Rock 5.8, Windows Section *Bego Gerhart*

George Hurley on the first ascent of Tonka Tower 5.8 A0, Windows Section *Earl Wiggins*

THE THREE GOSSIPS

Allen Steck had never been in the desert—let alone climbed there—and I thought it was about time he saw what it was like. Steck, I knew, would appreciate the desert, for he was a soulful person who craved beauty. He had also been mesmerized by Chuck Pratt's article in *Ascent* magazine, "The View from Dead Horse Point," which had appeared only months earlier. I insisted that our venture be more than just a climbing trip, and I had little argument.

Three of us drove in serpentine curves through Arizona and Utah, seeking nirvana. Pratt's message—that the desert was hard to appreciate, but eminently worth the trouble—was well founded, we discovered after a week or so of wandering. We saw buttes illuminated by magical lighting, and we watched dust devils swirl through the sagebrush. Near Dead Horse Point we watched a prairie falcon spear a luckless horned lark. And once, in a lost canyon in lost hills, a golden eagle banked so close to the windshield that we ducked.

The time finally came to climb, and I mentioned Arches as a place where short, undiscovered routes were as abundant as the beer cans alongside the highways of Navajoland. I was pointing out the sights when Steck said, "Has *that* been climbed?" I hardly had to look to answer in the negative, for virtually nothing had yet been climbed. Kor, in his halcyon days, had visited the place, I knew, but had done only a climb or two.

We stared at the Three Gossips, a 250-foot-high pillar with, naturally, three summits. Silence. "Maybe there's a route on the other side," I said. "Let's go look," Steck said.

The side opposite the road *did* have a crack system, a good one for Steck's first desert lead, I thought. He pounded pins up the long initial crack for hours, it seemed. Once in a while he would yell down: "I wonder if this one's any good?" I would yell back: "It's up to you, man, but, hell, didn't you hear it ring?" Meanwhile, I braced myself to catch a fall, for sandstone was not granite, and a ring in the one was not the same as a ring in the other.

The pins shifted and creaked as I followed, but none popped, a testimony to Steck's skill—or beginner's luck. Higher, near the top, it was again his turn, and he did a masterful job of finding a 5.7 route onto the highest summit. As I recall, this crack, though moderate, was intimidating and unprotected—a bold end to our insignificant first ascent.

As it turned out, this was the only time we roped up during the three-week trip. We had learned to put our ropes away and wander through the slickrock in order to appreciate the Four Corners. We had, without any difficulty, followed Pratt's credo, and we drove back to Berkeley with souls refreshed.

Steve Roper

Argon Tower, first ascent Kor collection

Bob Bradley, Layton Kor, and Charlie Kemp on the summit of Argon Tower, the first ascent Kor collection

COLORADO RIVER VALLEY

As the Colorado River flows slowly west from the Fisher Towers toward Moab, the surrounding expanse of outstretched ridges topped by red Wingate cliffs gradually narrows. Talus slopes shrink in size, and the Wingate becomes blocky, broken by a multitude of horizontal seams. The river valley constricts further as sheer, yellowish-pink walls of Navajo sandstone rise out of the river. Towering at 400 feet or more, these smooth walls with scalloped crests are undercut, increasing their imposing appearance. Brown and black water streaks add color and character as they cascade down the steep rock faces.

Small side creeks feeding the Colorado River have cut deep side canyons through this otherwise continuous fortress of slickrock. Numerous petroglyphs, pictographs, and other evidence of ancient life can be found in caves and along the walls of these side canyons.

As the Colorado River meanders farther west past Moab, the terrain begins to unfold. Slickrock fins appear. As the exposed Navajo sandstone becomes older and less formidable, the landscape becomes more broken and tiered. Side canyons spilling into the Colorado become more frequent. Soon broad canyons, rimmed with Wingate above long talus slopes, drop down to the river, signalling the start of Canyonlands National Park.

This brief section of the Colorado River drainage, from the Fisher Towers to Canyonlands National Park, contains numerous established climbs as well as infinite possibilities for new routes. Many climbers have driven through the river valley

BUSINESS REPLY MAIL

FIRST CLASS   PERMIT NO. 285   BOULDER, CO

POSTAGE WILL BE PAID BY:

PRUETT *P* **PUBLISHING COMPANY**

2928 Pearl Street • Boulder, Colorado 80301-9989

Thank you for your interest in one of our titles. Pruett Publishing publishes books in various fields, including outdoor recreation guides, western americana titles, and fine railroad books. If you would like a free catalog of our entire line of books, please fill out this postage-paid reply card.

Thank you.

Name: _____

Address: _____

City/State/Zip: _____

Area of particular interest:

☐ Western Americana

☐ Outdoor/Recreation Guides

☐ Railroads

☐ Other (please specify) _____

Climber's view of the Colorado River *Katy Cassidy*

and perhaps even camped beside its peaceful water. Yet relatively few have explored the miles and miles of canyon walls that stand guard over the slow and quiet river.

In April of 1969 Kor climbed Dolomite Tower, a 300-foot pinnacle above the Colorado River, with his wife, Joy, and nephew, Kordell. This was to be Kor's last new route in the Moab area. His remarkable drive led him in other directions through the following years. Climbing became less important to Kor, yet his legacy of first ascents are still of great importance to climbing. Many of his desert routes have become classics, and a few still remain unrepeated. His impact on the sport is unforgettable, and it serves as an inspiration to those who follow in his steps through the labyrinth of canyons here in the Southwest.

The early seventies saw the first real activity in the river valley. Harvey Carter added to his long list of first ascents by ascending Lighthouse Tower, Dolomite's neighbor, in May 1970. Climbing with Gary Ziegler and Tom Merrill, Carter pushed the route up four difficult pitches, only to be confronted by a blank summit headwall. The trio showed determination when they threw a rope up and over the top and boldly jumared to the untouched summit. This precarious maneuver has since been eliminated.

Several short free climbs were established in a concentrated area near Sheep Canyon, just upriver from Moab, in the first few years of the seventies. To this day they remain popular due to their moderate grade and nonexistent approach. Also in the Sheep Canyon area are three particularly good mixed routes of longer length. Split Pillar, completed in 1972 by Jon Hall and Muff Cheney, ascends a huge open book. This multipitch route is notable as it was the first mixed climb in the area.

In the next canyon east, Negro Bill Flake was climbed in 1974. Combining A4 aid climbing with 5.11 off-widthing, this route was considered a test

Dolomite and Lighthouse towers *Earl Wiggins*

Jeff Achey on the first ascent of Iron Maiden 5.11 A3, Lighthouse Tower *Ed Webster*

piece for many years. This fine route is capped off with a "leaping mantle" from the main wall to the flake's summit. The leap across a six-foot-wide chasm to a 5.10 mantle is, to say the least, very intimidating. Failure on either the leap or the mantle results in an awful plunge into the dark depths of the bottomless flake.

The boldest route in the area is without doubt Artist Tears. This serious route follows bottoming seams up a soft and severely overhanging Navajo sandstone wall for three pitches. Attempted several times in the early seventies, Artist Tears received its first ascent by Larry Bruce and Molly Higgins in May of 1976. At the time of its establishment, this route represented the cutting edge of desert nailing. Faced with the likelihood of hitting the ground should she fall, Molly moved steadily up the first pitch.

Higgins's journal reads, "May 25—I 'won' a coin toss for the first pitch and got to lead it. Super intimidated, it seemed ridiculous for me to be heading up on something so hard. The first pitch involved face moves to a bolt, hook moves to another bolt, dowels and bolts to a roof, then 80 feet of A4 to the belay. A4 is so intense you don't even whimper or whine, just get very quiet." Climbing a pitch a day, they completed the route on May 27, elated and proud. Since Artist Tears has only received a few repeat ascents in the following years, the pair's fears of having the climb become beat out seems comical in retrospect. Higgins's journal describes these fears and her impressions of Artist Tears. "A beautiful thin line winding up the painted and overhanging smooth sandstone face on the Colorado River. It's a line that will quickly get beat out. But we are possessed and possessive and we want the route. . . . When Larry heard that the route would be a first ascent he became mad, impatient with other climbs, he only wanted to get to the Colorado River."

The climbs of the seventies were a mere scratch on the surface compared to the potential that the river canyon held. Here as elsewhere, the eighties saw an explosion in activity. Ed Webster and Jeff Achey attacked Lighthouse Tower in 1985 and 1986, establishing several fine routes. Achey, strong in body and mind, led the second pitch on Iron Maiden. This wild pitch has since turned back several top climbers. His boldness and imagination resulted in a lead consisting of creative stemming for thirty feet up a blank, desert varnished corner to an overhanging headwall. Achey hung on with one arm and beat a piton into a horizontal seam before proceeding to hand traverse across the smooth, steep wall for twenty-five feet, finally reaching a thin finger crack in a vertical corner. The corner led up to another hand traverse, after which Achey finally decided to establish a belay. The pitch is serious, demanding, and one of the most beautiful in the desert.

In the mid-eighties attention focused on areas downriver from Moab. The wealth of climbing potential right off the Potash Highway was quickly recognized. The Potash Road offered a new twist to desert climbing: face climbing. Other notable face routes had appeared here and there through-

Jason Keith soloing Artist Tears V A4, Anasazi Wall *Katy Cassidy*

Larry Bruce on the second pitch, first ascent of Artist Tears V A4, Anasazi Wall *Molly Higgins*

Peter Gallagher and Bego Gerhart on the King's Hand 5.10, Potash Road *Earl Wiggins*

Craig Leuben on the first ascent of Offwidths are Beautiful 5.10, Potash Road *Earl Wiggins*

out the desert, but Potash was the first area that solely concentrated on face routes. With few exceptions, most Potash routes are short, technically difficult, and quite enjoyable. Unfortunately, being so close to the road can be very annoying. The optimal time to climb these routes is in the winter when the traffic is minimal and the rock is sheltered from cold winds and warmed by the winter sun.

Farther downriver where the Entrada disappears and the Wingate begins to tower above the ambling river, Long Canyon strikes off to the north. Many exceptional crack climbs were established in this stunning canyon in the late eighties. With spectacular views of the La Sal Mountains and a quiet atmosphere, Long Canyon offers easy access to quality climbs while avoiding the traffic of Potash Road.

Dead Horse Point, a peninsula of rock jutting out from the Island in the Sky mesa, was often used to corral wild horses. Requiring only a small fence to secure the animals from escaping north onto the mesa, this natural corral was used frequently by early cowboys. The point received its name when a group of horses was abandoned, locked inside the corral, and left to die of thirst while the Colorado River flowed in plain view 2000 feet below.

In 1978 Ron Olevsky soloed a five-pitch route on the cliff below Dead Horse Point when his partner was unable at the last minute to join him. To facilitate the return to his car once he had finished the climb, Olevsky left his off-road bicycle

at the top before descending down the rough four-wheel-drive roads into the river canyon.

After completing the long, demanding route and mounting his bicycle for the return into the river canyon, Olevsky was asked by several bewildered tourists where his partner was. Without thinking, he replied that his partner "was unable to make it." As he rode off, Olevsky glanced over his shoulder and saw the tourists gazing over the edge, horrified, searching the depths below for the body.

The climbing in the Colorado River drainage and its side canyons is unique unto itself. The rock is often soft, blocky, and questionable. The views of the river add a dimension to desert climbing that is not often found in many of the other areas of the Southwest. With 90 percent of the river canyon accessible only by water, river running might become the transportation of future climbers wishing to venture deeper into the canyon country. However, the Moab area offers easy access to several miles of the mighty river without a boat. A good strenuous climb and a cool dip in the placid water should not be missed by those visiting this region.

The La Sals rising above slickrock domes *Earl Wiggins*

Carol Petrelli on Necro Dancer 5.10+, Long Canyon *Katy Cassidy*

The Monitor *Katy Cassidy*

Peter Gallagher finishing off the Plunge 5.12, Monitor Butte *Earl Wiggins*

60

The first pitch of the Plunge 5.12, Monitor Butte *Katy Cassidy*

The first pitch of the Prow of the Merrimac 5.11 A0, Merrimac Butte *Katy Cassidy*

The first pitch of Keel Hauling 5.9, Merrimac Butte
Katy Cassidy

The first pitch of Stand and Deliver 5.11, Merrimac Butte *Earl Wiggins*

Petroglyphs *Katy Cassidy*

THE DESERT

Sandstone towers gracefully concede
to the sculptor called time.
Jealously guarded by talus slopes,
and cactus flowers that sparkle through the dust
like sapphires nestled in jade,
their cracks connect earth and sky.
The smells of freshly crushed sage
and broken, dried up junipers
mingle among the cringing old cottonwoods.
Reminders of the water that once was,
they welcome us home.

MONICA LOU/CHIP CHACE

CANYONLANDS ROCK

On my first rock climbing trip to Canyonlands, the handful of previously established desert climbs were all located on the region's most prominent pinnacles: Castleton Tower, the Priest, and Moses, among others. Yet on the literally hundreds of miles of Wingate cliffs, hardly a single climb had been attempted, much less completed to the top of a mesa. Scarcely did I know what an enthralling and formative experience awaited me on those red canyon walls. I had never seen a single picture of those fabled cracks, but the vivid descriptions of them by my friends filled my imagination to overflowing . . .

ED WEBSTER

Kordell Kor on the first ascent of Dolomite Tower Kor collection

65

CANYONLANDS NATIONAL PARK

Sunset on Moses *Ed Webster*

West of Moab is Canyonlands National Park, 527 square miles of the most rugged, inaccessible country on the Colorado Plateau. In the northern half of Canyonlands National Park, the Green River to the west and the Colorado River to the east both journey diagonally south toward their confluence. These deep, broad river gorges have carved a triangular chunk of land between them. This exposed mesa, aptly named Island in the Sky, is rather whole toward its north end, but south toward the confluence, the number of drainages carving deep canyons on their way to the rivers below multiplies. This sculpting of the land creates a network of peninsulas that branch off into yet more crooked fingers of land. Off these points, hidden within this extensive maze of canyons, are exquisite Wingate towers. Tall, with an average height of 600 feet, steep, and solid with excellent crack systems, these towers don't give away their summits easily.

A few rough roads lead down off Island in the Sky to the White Rim. The Shafer Trail is one of them. Initially the Shafer Trail was a narrow foot trail circumnavigating the abutment of sheer sandstone walls below Island in the Sky. Cowboys used to drive their herds of cattle down this steep trail on their way to the Green River. This small trail, which has since been enlarged into a two-wheel-drive road characterized by sharp curves and gut-wrenching dropoffs, is a credit to its founder's amazing route-finding abilities.

Once at the White Rim, the Shafer Trail connects with the White Rim Road. This 110-mile dirt road travels along a shelf of solid white sandstone as it traces the perimeter of Island in the Sky. Contouring into canyons and back out around points of land, this tedious, bumpy road offers access to the huge talus slopes and canyons leading up to the Wingate spires and buttes of Canyonlands.

Below Grandview Point, the southern tip of Island in the Sky, the protective shelf of dense, white rim sandstone has fallen away, exposing Monument Basin. This large concave niche is distinguished by a myriad of crumbling Cutler sandstone towers. Appearing to defy gravity, these 350-foot, deep red and purple towers are a rare sight in the national park. Here, as in other parts of the park, only a few of the spires have been climbed. The vast, rugged terrain of Canyonlands has greatly inhibited access to climbs, leaving countless cliffs, buttes, and canyons yet to be explored. Noted author and preservationist Ed Abbey accurately describes Canyonlands National Park as "the least inhabited, least inhibited, least developed, least improved, least civilized . . . most arid, most hostile, most lonesome, most grim, bleak, barren, desolate, and savage quarter of the state of Utah—the best part by far."

Spires such as those found in Canyonlands are the essence of the great American Southwest. Their likeness has appeared repeatedly in artwork depicting landscapes of the region. In a visual format, they embody all that is the Southwest: Indians, cowboys, rugged land, and a subtle connection to the ancient past.

Even though in the 1980s climbing spread to the buttes, mesas, and canyon walls, it was the spires

Climbers on the summit of Moses *Stewart Green*

alone that were the focal point in the late fifties through to the mid-seventies. For nearly twenty years the numerous untouched summits beckoned a small but determined group of individuals from many parts of the country. They came, again and again, searching for the illusive towers.

In the article, "The View From Dead Horse Point," in the 1970 *Ascent* magazine, Chuck Pratt writes, "Why the desert should exert such a fascination on a handful of climbers is a mystery to those who are not attracted to it, for the climbs in the Four Corners, with a few exceptions, have little to recommend them. They are generally short— often requiring less time than the approaches, the rock at its best is brittle and rotten and at its worst is the consistency of sugar."

It was indeed a mystery to most climbers as to what could possibly be attractive about the area. Only the individuals who were active there during those twenty years knew the answer. Part of the

attraction was the slender, delicate spires that were found nowhere else on earth. Part was the surrounding environment that shielded, blanketed, and imprisoned the numerous towers. The environment itself was a source of adventure, sometimes severe, for those who penetrated its depths.

Cars were abused. Hours and sometimes days were spent recreating roads. Wallets were emptied paying for car repairs. And many times climbs were never even reached. Yet these trips were declared successful.

Simply being in the desert was as rewarding as the climbing itself. The maze of canyons imprisoning the spires is brimming with peril, an ingredient helpful in creating adventure.

One by one the spires were picked off through the fifties, sixties, and seventies. There are still countless smaller formations, and possibly well-hidden larger ones, but the obvious towers have been ascended. After a long dormant period following the successful 1939 ascent of Shiprock, situated in northern New Mexico, attention focused on three specific spires located on the Navajo Reservation. Spider Rock, Cleopatra's Needle, and the Totem Pole were climbed in quick succession in the late fifties. These three ascents by a California group were the genesis for modern desert climbing.

In the early sixties, Layton Kor made repeat ascents of the Californian routes after completing first ascents of Castleton and the Priest. He then began a decade of searching out and climbing as many towers as his time allowed. Through the sixties Kor climbed more than twenty major towers, and most were first ascents. His partners were almost as numerous as his ascents. Their regard

Pete Carmen leading on the first ascent of Washer Woman, IV 5.8 A3
Rick Horn collection

Descending from Washer Woman *Alison Sheets*

Art Wiggins jumaring on the first ascent of Sharks Fin,
V A4 *Earl Wiggins*

Standing Rock *Charlie Fowler*

72

for Kor as a climber was extremely high, yet their relief at living through such horrendous climbs was even greater. To each it seemed a miracle that they should survive these harrowing endeavors.

In October of 1962 Steve Komito and Huntley Ingalls joined Kor for the first ascent of Standing Rock, a formation that Komito says resembles "layers of Rye Crisp held together by moistened kitty litter." At the time, this was one of the most difficult towers to approach. Making the road passable to Komito's new station wagon required major road work. In *Beyond The Vertical* Komito recounts, "I relinquished the helm of my little car to Layton when my will to go forward had fettered at the second incidence of high centering, only a few miles off the paved highway from Moab. Kor had ended my whining protests by growling 'You don't think we're gonna turn back now that we're this close do you?' I hoped weakly that we would, but resigned myself to sitting in back gripping the seat as if I could somehow lift the rear wheels gently over the rows of ruts arrayed ahead of us like the sabers of an enemy host."

On Monster Tower, a 650-foot Wingate monolith, Larry Dalke and Cub Schafer found themselves in subfreezing temperatures while Kor led higher and higher. It was the day after Christmas 1963. Ledges were covered with snow, and cracks were lined with ice. Dalke and Schafer sat in long, uncomfortable belays on the north face, out of reach of the winter sun.

The list of tales is endless. Most of Kor's partners can remember how he would dramatically depict the worst aspect of every situation. Listening to talk of belay pins shifting, imminent long falls, and whole towers that might fall down during a climb were all part of teaming up with Kor. George Hurley, a close friend and frequent partner, claims Kor was a master at securing the lead by creating incredible fear and doubt in his partners.

One very notable ascent was of Washer Woman by Rick Horn, John Horn, and Peter Carmen. This precarious neighbor of Monster Tower required careful routefinding and equipment supplemented with wooden wedges and an ice piton. Both Monster and Washer Woman were unrepeated until the early 1980s.

By the early seventies, desert spires were attracting a larger following. Though still a definite subculture of mainstream climbing, soft-rock routes were gaining popularity. Several new towers were located and climbed during the first few years of the decade.

Most noteworthy was Moses. Perched atop an impressive scree cone and surrounded by the sheer walls of Taylor Canyon, Moses is tucked deep into the northern part of Canyonlands. Several attempts were made by Eric Bjørnstad and Fred Beckey to climb the huge tower. Determined to reach the summit, they returned a final time with five climbers and engaged in expedition tactics. After five days of cold, wet weather, they managed to push a route up the north face and onto the top. The route, now known as Pale Fire, goes all free and is often climbed on hot summer days by climbers seeking shelter from the blistering sun.

The late seventies brought a renewed interest in the desert spires, this time to establish free routes.

Peter Gallagher contemplating the second pitch on Standing Rock, 5.7 A3
Art Wiggins

Climbers on Pale Fire, 5.12, Moses *Stewart Green*

Aid climbing was no longer required to gain the tops of many of the towers. Free climbing, which is often much speedier than aid, allowed many of the towers that had previously been climbed in two or more days to now be ascended in one. This brought a noticeable increase in the number of climbers visiting the area. Spires such as Zeus, Moses, Monster, Washer Woman, and Candlestick became well known among a new and larger group of climbers.

Perhaps the most popular route in Canyonlands National Park is the Primrose Dihedrals on Moses. This elegant climb was first ascended by Ed Webster, solo, in the spring of 1979. Realizing the route would provide superb free climbing, Webster returned with Steve Hong in the fall. Their free ascent was another step toward combining beautiful Wingate free climbing with desert summits. However, there are still several summits attainable only by aid climbing, such as Standing Rock, Sharks Fin, Islet, and Blocktop. A small handful of climbers still enjoy the abundant aid climbing in the desert. For them, there are countless routes left to accomplish.

In the forefront of aid development in the park, Ron Olevsky has explored numerous side canyons and hidden corners along the Green River. He has found and climbed many previously unknown towers. His multiple endeavors have been aided by canoe, plane, dynamite, his four-wheel-drive truck, and his loyal companion, a pup named Bat Hook.

Although we as climbers seek out summits, it is perhaps more often true that our rewards are gained from the overall experience. The desert spires are magnificent to behold and exhilarating to stand atop, but it is in the journey itself that one comes to know and love the Canyon Country.

In his article on the Bride, Eric Bjørnstad writes, "The desert, not unlike the Himalaya, the Alps, or the Bugaboos, compels with a type of magical adoration. The world there is its own, demanding its particular respects, offering its rewards. At once luring and repelling; addicting its trespassers to its treasures. Temperatures are seldom right. Often unbearably hot, or unpredictably cold. Frequently running the gamut within the few hours before and after dusk, before and after dawn. Only brief days of spring and fall offer passable climbing conditions. And then the eyes are subject to pain from sand-filled air and food is unavoidably gritty. High winds can whip the climbing rope to threads in hours and bring communication to a frustrating halt. The climber usually knows on his first trip whether the reward-effort is in balance for him and whether or not he is likely to return. There are rigors too humorous to tell. But there is something else there, the quiet, the majesty, grandeur — more notable than I have experienced anywhere."

Cub Schafer, Larry Dalke, and Layton Kor on the summit of Monster Tower, the first ascent *Kor collection*

Ed Webster on the first free ascent of Primrose Dihedrals 5.11, Moses
Steve Hong

Kelly Carignan on Primrose Dihedrals 5.11, Moses *Bob Rotert*

Spring storm in the canyon country *Earl Wiggins*

THE VALUE OF AUDACITY

Something that has never ceased to amaze me when it comes to getting up new routes in the desert is the value of audacity. Many of those climbs look so ridiculous that for me talent seemed purely secondary to having the right vision. That attitude of "What the hell, it's probably impossible, but let's slog up the talus cone and have a look." And so many of those routes turn out to be perfectly reasonable.

I can remember rapping down the north face of Moses and having Jeff tell me that the bolt ladder would never go. That part of it went at 5.8 in the rain. On that same trip we were looking at Sisyphus on Zeus; the first pitch looked patently impossible to me. Later

that fall Jeff hauled me up it with ease. We used to joke that the size of a desert crack was never fixed in reality until we'd climbed it, because we'd always get suckered. When we were on Sacred Space we looked over at this incredible crack in an overhanging wall on Hummingbird Spire and figured it would be inch and a quarter at best, or some nasty size like that, and we were only seventy feet away looking straight across at it. Jeff later went back and did it. It was perfect hands. Things are never what they seem.

CHIP CHACE

John Horn and Pete Carmen on the summit of Washer Woman, the first ascent *Rick Horn*

Larry Dalke on the first ascent of Monster Tower *Kor collection*

INDIAN CREEK

Springtime at Indian Creek. *Katy Cassidy*

Driving west off highway 191, steep switchbacks lead down from wide open sagebrush country to the fertile valley of Indian Creek. This long valley, narrow at its southeast end, quickly broadens toward the northwest. Endless cliffs of vertical Wingate sandstone, 300 feet high, enclose the valley, contour into shallow cul-de-sacs, and form the walls of extensive side canyons. The rock throughout the area is in varying stages of erosion, with colors ranging from pale yellow and white to all shades of red, orange, and pink. Still, the majority of rock is high quality—deep red with a veneer of desert varnish. This smooth veneer is highly reflective, shining deep blue and black on sunny days.

Below the cliffs is a relatively short apron of light-colored scree, offering easy access to the walls above. Hidden among the odd large boulders in the talus slopes and along the lower sections of the cliffs are the remains of ancient Indian dwellings. Also found along the base of the cliffs are numerous petroglyphs pecked into the desert varnish.

Down in the valley, overgrown cottonwood trees follow Indian Creek as it winds its way along the valley floor, adding bright colors to the fall and deep greens to the spring scenery. Cows graze in broad pastures next to irrigated fields bright green with alfalfa. The abundance of hardy sage bushes imparts a delicate scent to the air.

This peaceful valley, unsullied by human impact, nurtures a friendly atmosphere and makes for lots of fun climbing.

The first climbers to visit Indian Creek came searching for spires. The seemingly endless canyon walls split by thousands of cracks failed to capture their interest. North and South Six-shooter spires were found and quickly climbed. Today South Six-shooter is rarely climbed due to its small size and fairly long approach. For climbers looking for short, enjoyable, and moderate climbs it can't be beat.

North Six-shooter is much more formidable, with steep, clean cracks splitting its sheer Wingate walls. This tower is probably climbed more often than any other spire except Castleton. Most visiting climbers are drawn to the classic Lightning Bolt Cracks. This route is a desert test piece that offers almost every size of crack climbing imaginable.

In 1962 Steve Komito, Rick Horn, and Huntley Ingalls attempted a route on the southeast flanks of North Six-shooter. Although forced to retreat due to fierce winds and an accompanying sandstorm, they returned the following day to try once again. The second attempt went smoothly, and they found themselves on top in the late afternoon sun. On the second rappel the ropes became jammed. After spending much time flipping, jiggling, and tugging, the ropes still would not come loose. "Komito and I held our breath as Rick prussiked up a single line to free it up," Huntley recounts in a letter to a friend. Fortunately Horn was successful. They were soon bounding down the great scree slopes toward the car with yet another desert first ascent to their credit.

In 1967 Steve Roper and Chuck Pratt made the

Jeff Widen, Tony Valdes on the Lightning Bolt cracks 5.11, North Six-shooter *Bego Gerhart*

Veronica Bleuze on Bunny Slope 5.9 *Bret Ruckman*

second ascent of the original route. While descending they spied another possible climb on the north face. Two years later Pratt found himself back at the base of North Six-shooter with Doug Robinson. Soaring above them was a breathtaking eight-inch crack, Pratt's specialty. A photo featured in *Ascent* magazine in 1970 enabled readers to gawk at Chuck on this impressive, unprotected lead. That photo alone struck fear in the hearts and minds of climbers contemplating a desert climbing trip.

Jeff Achey on the first ascent of Thumbelina 5.11, Bridger Jack group
Ed Webster

Over the next two decades this route remained a fearful undertaking. Like Twilight Zone in Yosemite, Pratt's Crack is a testimony to his understated ability to run it out. With the invention of wide-crack protection such as BigBros, this climb has since become an enjoyable classic. Of course, those who want to experience the original style can just leave their rack on the ground.

In the early seventies Jim Dunn visited and climbed North Six-shooter. Trends in climbing throughout the United States were swinging more toward free climbing. While driving through Indian Creek on his way to North Six-shooter, Dunn took more than a passing interest in the thousands of perfect cracks lining the canyon walls. He returned repeatedly through the following years. At first he came only to walk along the base of the walls and stare, but eventually he attempted many of the awesome fissures.

There were two enormous differences in climbing at Indian Creek in the seventies compared to the eighties. First, the idea of establishing routes that didn't go to the top of the mesa was inconceivable. Routes that stopped part way were not given a second look, thus limiting the scope of climbing in the area. Steve Hong broke through this old school tradition in the eighties and established uncountable high-quality routes. Indeed, in the eighties the pendulum swung in the opposite direction. It became rare to find routes that were longer than a rope length.

Perhaps the most limiting factor of the seventies was protection, or more precisely the lack of protection. Before the invention of Friends in the

Jim Nigro on Painted Pony, 5.11 *Katy Cassidy*

Charlie Fowler on Johnny Cat 5.12 *Katy Cassidy*

late seventies, Indian Creek cracks were not just physically demanding, they were also very serious ventures. Closely following the trend toward free climbing in this country was the trend toward clean climbing. The first active climbers at Indian Creek didn't carry pins or for that matter even bolt kits. Armed only with racks of Chouinard hexes, which were terrific in other areas but almost useless in the parallel-sided cracks, it was not uncommon to be forced to run it out sixty, eighty, or even a hundred feet at a time.

This era has been affectionately named "Before Friends." Dunn had only a handful of partners during these years. Without leaving a trace of their passing, this small group climbed many routes, all to the top of the cliff. Some of these routes have become classics; many have merely been forgotten.

One particular side canyon derived its name from the forced runout on an unforgettable first ascent attempt. Fringe of Death Canyon, named after a particularly dicey lead, became the focus of attention in the early seventies. The name was coined by Jim Dunn while belaying a young partner of his on a vertical fingertip layback up a smooth black wall split by a parallel-sided one-inch crack. Equipped with many small hexcentrics, the leader laybacked higher and higher, trying desperately to get a nut placement. Stopping every few feet and hanging off of one arm, the young climber tried frantically to establish protection.

The hexs were useless in the smooth crack. "I thought we had finally overstepped our limits," says Dunn. "He was getting further and further out. No rests anywhere in sight and not a single

Jim Nigro riding the Wave 5.10 *Earl Wiggins*

Charlie Fowler having at Crack Attack 5.10 *Katy Cassidy*

Sunset on Crack Attack *Earl Wiggins*

Lisa Gnade firing off Coynes Crack 5.12 *Katy Cassidy*

piece between him and the ground. This was really the fringe of death. I didn't know if I should clear a landing or try to catch him when he came off. I was sure he wasn't going to make it and knew he couldn't downclimb."

Seventy feet above the ground a small stance appeared on the wall. With his last ounce of strength, the youngster swung up onto it. Dunn let out a deep sigh of relief as the sound of heavy breathing broke the quiet morning. A bolt was laboriously drilled for an escape to the ground. Fringe of Death became a name for that single climb, but to the small group of climbers, those three words epitomized climbing in Indian Creek.

Many fine routes were established in the following years by this band. Their tales of the purist crack climbing yet to be found fell on deaf ears whenever they traveled to other areas. However, in December of 1978 an article on desert climbing, specifically focusing on a particular climb in Indian Creek, appeared in *Mountain* magazine.

The author, Ed Webster, had given that certain climb a catchy name well suited for a glitzy magazine. First climbed in 1976 before Friends, Super Crack of the Desert has now become a well-known climb throughout the world. Its stark, crisp beauty attracts hundreds of ascents every year. Once those first pictures were published of Super Crack and other unrelenting climbs close by, people began to listen more closely to tales of the desert and even to contemplate investigating further into this well-kept secret.

Slowly at first, then more and more, people

came to see, feel, and attempt climbs. Friends were just becoming available, and though they were considered "new-fangled gadgetry," it was obvious they would be very important to the future development of Indian Creek. The era of "After Friends" began slowly, yet within a few years hundreds of new routes had been established. Though very expensive by old standards, people began to amass huge racks of Friends. On many of the more difficult routes it is now quite common to use ten to fifteen Friends of a certain size.

There have been several key figures in the area's development. Jim Dunn, Mugs Stump, Ed Webster, and Steve Hong were all active before and during the transition from Before Friends to After Friends. In the eighties many more climbers took interest, and activity spread throughout the numerous canyons. Ed Webster, Chip Chace, Jeff Achey, Peter Gallagher, Monica Lou, Anne Leibold, and Taras Skibicky pioneered long extreme routes on the Bridger Jack towers. This ridge of towers affords the best of Wingate climbing combined with true desert summits. Packed with a high concentration of multipitch crack climbs, this area has long been overlooked by the multitudes of climbers visiting Indian Creek.

Karin Budding on Tricks are for Kids 5.13+. No, the shoes don't fit. *Steve Hong*

Steve Hong on the first ascent of 9-Lives 5.11+ *Karin Budding*

Burton Moomaw cruising the Incredible Handcrack 5.10
Earl Wiggins

The main focus of interest throughout the eighties has been on the many miles of buttresses and canyon walls towering above State Highway 211. Steve Hong, one of Jim Dunn's original partners in the seventies, was without a doubt the most active climber throughout the seventies and eighties. Teamed with the very talented Karin Budding, this duo single-handedly picked off the best quality routes on almost every wall in the area. Climbers searching for untouched walls often complain of finding themselves beaten by this notorious pair. Their long list of first ascents is quite impressive, containing dozens of routes in each grade up to 5.13s. Steve calmly claims that he has never had any epics, yet says in the same breath, "Don't get me wrong, though. I think desert climbing is the most dangerous kind of climbing there is. I've come closer to getting the chop down here compared to anywhere else."

Although Hong and Budding have been in the forefront, many strong climbers have contributed to the fine assortment of routes. Indian Creek has become a great socializing area due to the ideal camping scene and the easy access to routes. It is still simple enough to avoid other people, yet many come specifically to Indian Creek to see friends from other parts of the country and the world.

At night when the air becomes crisp and cold, the faint smell of burning pinion hangs lightly in the clear desert sky. Climbers wander from campfire to campfire mingling, reliving the day's climbs, and recounting tales of past adventures. Experiences are shared and new plans are drawn for future climbs while the coyote's mournful howls echo through the dark canyons.

Those who are old enough are reminded of Camp 4 in Yosemite. For others it appears to be a life consisting of limitless crack climbing and unregulated camping, a life too idyllic to be true. The desert is here for everyone to experience and enjoy. Fortunately, most of it is still open and not subject to rules, regulations, and fees. By being responsible for the care and nurturing of this fragile environment, we as climbers, a group disinclined to be regulated, can keep the desert clean and fresh for others to experience.

Craig Leuben cutting teeth on The Big Baby 5.11 *Katy Cassidy*

Keith Gotschall on Los Hermanos 5.12 *Earl Wiggins*

Karin Budding on the chopper hand traverse on R-Rated 5.11
Steve Hong

Keith Gotschall powering up Quarter of a Man 5.11 *Katy Cassidy*

Karin Budding on the first ascent of King Cat 5.11+ *Steve Carruthers*

Kelly Carignan on King Cat 5.11 *Bob Rotert*

Cactus in bloom *Steve Hong*

INDIAN CREEK

When I think of the desert my first reaction is to become sentimental. Probably the best days of my life, so far, have been spent exploring the canyon walls, climbing those amazing cracks, and sitting around the campfire at night with Steve and other friends. The amazing part about the place is that, snowstorms and stuck vehicles notwithstanding, these wonderful weekend trips have been repeated over and over—and there are still "5 stars" to be done.

Being the selfish person that I am and having gotten spoiled by the place being relatively empty for so long, it's been a little difficult watching Indian Creek become so popular the last few years. But it's a unique and beautiful area, and anyone who spends enough time there will soon come to love and respect it.

KARIN BUDDING

DIRT FEST

What to do in the desert with approximately two sets of Friends (mostly hand-sized and smaller—no #4) and a set of BigBros? Vision Quest, Chip had been told, was excellent, really varied in size (no mega-rack needed), all the loose blocks had been cleaned off it, and the crux was a .10c hand crack through a bulge. Sounded perfect.

After a finger crack, a sandy off-width to a sandy chimney, I emerged as the monster from the red dihedral. Or was this becoming one with the environment? A hand crack to another off-width/lieback that sucked up our biggest BigBro at the bottom led to a great stance atop the second pitch—if we'd had #4 Friends. We settled instead for a cramped semi-hanging belay where the crack was small enough to fit our rack.

Lacking big enough pro, Chip ran out the forty-foot, four-and-a-half-inch crack above, past loose flakes and chockstones to another off-width. The crux hand-crack through a bulge led to more chimneying. As I followed, it started to rain. Fortunately, rain just sort of soaks into the sandstone instead of sitting on the surface and making it slick. The last pitch had the requisite mantle into a papier-mache band followed by a long traverse through it, creating so much rope drag on the final crack I had to haul up armloads of slack just to make it to another stance so I could haul up more slack. Placing pro made it even worse, so I didn't. Once on the summit, we added our votes for the moniker "Dirt Fest" and rapped off, eager for baths in the creek.

MONICA LOU

Peter Gallagher on the summit of Bridger Jack, the first ascent Ed Webster

Rick Horn on the summit of North Six-shooter, the first ascent
Rick Horn collection

99